FIFE'S EARLY ARCHAEOLOGICAL
HERITAGE - A GUIDE

Fife Regional Council
Dunfermline District Council
Kirkcaldy District Council
North East Fife District Council

ISBN

Printed by Fife Regional Council, Glenrothes

PREFACE

This Guide to the Early Archaeology of Fife is a direct result of the work carried out by the Fife Sites and Monuments Record Project. The Project, funded jointly by Fife Regional Council, Dunfermline, Kirkcaldy and North East Fife District Councils, and the Manpower Services Commission, was set up under the Community Programme to compile a computer listing of the Archaeological Sites and Monuments Record in Fife. The Project ran for 2 years, and a basic Sites and Monuments Record for Fife now exists.

One of the original intentions of the Project was to make the Archaeology of Fife more widely known. This Guide is one of the first steps in achieving this. The information in the Guide is drawn from the Fife Sites and Monuments Record, as are most of the illustrations. The text of the Guide was primarily written by the Project Supervisor of the Fife Sites and Monuments Record Project, Miss Nicola Murray, to whom the sponsors are indebted. Editing has been carried out by the Department of Economic Development and Planning. The Guide is published jointly by Fife Regional Council, Dunfermline District Council, Kirkcaldy District Council, and North East Fife District Council, sponsors of the Project.

The publishers would also like to thank the following for their work and support in the publication of the Guide:-

The Fife Archaeological Index, The Royal Commission on the Ancient and Historical Monuments of Scotland, Scottish Development Department (Historic Buildings and Monuments), The Royal Museum of Scotland, Glenrothes Development Corporation.

Further information, and advice on other archaeological sites in Fife, is available from the Fife Sites and Monuments Record, Department of Economic Development and Planning, Fife Regional Council, Fife House, North Street, Glenrothes, Fife, KY7 5LT, tel: Glenrothes (0592) 754411

Acknowledgements

The Publishers wish to thank the following for permission to reproduce their photographs as illustrations:

Dunfermline District Council
Kirkcaldy District Council
North East Fife District Council
The Royal Commission on the Ancient and Historical Monuments of Scotland
The Royal Museum of Scotland

CONTENTS

INTRODUCTION

Fife has a great wealth of archaeological sites which form our legacy from the many peoples who have inhabited the region over the last 9,000 years. Each successive generation has left its mark on the landscape in the form of camp-sites, settlements, and cemeteries. These sites vary greatly in their form and nature. At one extreme they may consist of little more than a scatter of flint tools. At the other extreme they may be deserted villages abandoned in antiquity.

Some archaeological sites are still visible as upstanding monuments but many more lie hidden beneath the soil. The preservation of a site depends largely on the materials which were used in its construction and the location of the site in the modern landscape. Structures which were built of wood are very rarely found. Wood, like other organic materials, decays rapidly and will only be preserved under waterlogged or exceptionally dry conditions. Stone survives indefinitely, however, and some of Fife's ancient stone buildings have survived more or less intact. Sites constructed from earthen banks and mounds may also still be seen in the upland areas of the region. On good agricultural land, however, generations of farmers have ploughed such sites away.

Although few upstanding archaeological sites are visible in the lowland farming areas of the region, many sites may still be discovered from the air as cropmarks on aerial photographs. These cropmarks are caused by the walls or ditches of former settlements which are buried beneath the soil. Hard features, such as buried walls, cause the ripening crop to grow shorter and to turn yellow earlier. In contrast, buried ditches hold additional moisture and will allow the crop to grow taller and ripen later. Numerous cropmark sites have been discovered in Fife and they greatly enhance our knowledge of the prehistoric landscape.

Excavation of an archaeological site will reveal ancient structures and will often produce the remains of bones and pottery, hearths and tools. Analysis of these finds enables archaeologists to reconstruct a picture of ancient lifestyles and to investigate ways in which human society has changed over the centuries. Excavation by its very nature is a destructive process, however, and nowadays investigation is usually only carried out if the site is threatened by development. Where possible these splendid ancient monuments are now being preserved for the enjoyment of generations to come.

This booklet is intended as a guide to the archaeology of Fife. Part One is a general introduction which outlines the prehistory and history of the region. Part Two is a selected gazetteer of some of the upstanding monuments which may still be visited, studied and marvelled at today. The sites which have been included represent only a small fraction of Fife's archaeological resource, and specifically encludes industrial archaeology.

Each of the monuments described in Part II has been included on the map at the back of the book. In addition, the location of each site is described in relation to the Ordnance Survey 1:50,000 Landranger maps. Each entry in the gazetteer includes the relevant mapsheet number and the national grid reference of the site.

Some of the sites which are included in this guide are open to the public but many lie on private ground. Details of access arrangements are included with each site description.

For some sites, a more detailed guide may be available. This applies particularly to sites in the care of the Secretary of State for Scotland and National Trust Properties. For further information see the addresses at the back of this guide.

Visitors are reminded to follow the **Country Code:**

> Guard against all risk of fire
> Leave no litter
> Fasten all gates
> Safeguard water supplies
> Keep dogs under proper control
> Protect wildlife, wild plants and trees
> Keep to the paths across land
> Go carefully on country roads
> Avoid damaging fences, hedges and
>   walls
> Respect the life to the countryside

Many of Fife's museums have displays relating to the local archaeology of the area. A list of museums is included at the back of the Guide.

Part One

The Archaeology of Fife

Sites referred to in the text but not included in Part Two are given a national grid reference number.

Where a site is included in Part Two, it is given the appropriate reference number.

THE ARCHAEOLOGY OF FIFE

Hunters and Gatherers:
7,000 - 4,000 B C

People began to live in Scotland some 9,000 years ago, shortly after the end of the Ice Age. Scotland at this time was covered in dense woodland, which supported many varieties of game. The earliest inhabitants hunted these wild animals. They also caught fish and collected berries, wild fruits and other plants. As a result of the need to follow wild herds the first inhabitants did not build permanent villages but instead moved around from season to season, setting up temporary camps.

The presence of these early hunters in Fife may be recognised from the chance discovery of tools made from red deer antler. Such implements have been found at Broomhall near Limekilns and on the island of Inchkeith in the Firth of Forth. A series of temporary camp-sites have also been discovered at the farm of Morton on the edge of Tentsmuir in North East Fife (NO 467 227).

Morton was originally an island which was linked to the mainland only at low tide. It was an ideal place for catching sea-birds, shell-fish and deep-water fish such as cod, haddock and turbot. The site was excavated in the 1950's when traces of hearths, shelters and man-made wind-breaks were found. Radiocarbon dating of charcoal from some of the hearths showed that people had lived on the island at several different times between 7,000 and 6,000 B.C.

First Farmers & Metalworkers:
4,000 - 600 B.C.

Around 4,000 B.C. a new way of life was introduced to the British Isles - farming. Settlers from Europe brought with them cereal crops and domesticated animals. They also brought new techniques and skills. They made tools of polished stone and fired clay in ovens to produce pottery bowls and jars. Archaeologists use the term "Neolithic" to describe this period in prehistory. Translated literally, it means the New Stone Age.

Farming was often a very successful way of life and was quickly adopted by the local hunters and gatherers. Freed from the need to follow wild herds, these early farmers settled in villages and constructed permanent homes. The houses of these "Neolithic" farmers in Fife were probably built of wood and thatch. These perishable materials decay quickly and few traces remain. However early farming communities also built structures using earth and stone, materials which are better able to withstand the ravages of time. The structures which survive in Fife fall into three categories - henges, stone circles and cist burials.

Henges are found throughout Britain from Dorset in the south to the Northern Isles. They consist of a deep circular ditch surrounded by an earthen bank. The area thus enclosed forms a wide platform, upon which circles of timber posts or standing stones were occasionally erected. Access to the platform interior was gained by one or two causeways cut across the bank and ditch. A fine example of such a henge monument has been excavated at Balfarg (1). Radiocarbon dates from this site of around 3,000 B.C. confirm that farming communities were well established in Fife by this time.

Henges are thought to have been the meeting places of local farming communities, providing a place to gather for ceremonies and ritual activities. They also represent a considerable investment of time and labour. The farmers had only simple tools such as antler mattocks and stone picks with which to dig the ditches and move great mounds of earth. It can be imagined therefore, that the construction of a henge required the co-operation and combined effort of a whole community.

Similar communal organisation must also have been required in the construction of the second type of Neolithic monument, stone circles. In the 18th and 19th centuries these puzzling structures were described as "Druidical temples". Archaeological investigation has revealed that the circles were erected not by "Druids", but by our early farming ancestors. We may only speculate as to the function of these circles but it seems possible that they formed the prehistoric equivalent of later churches and cathedrals - centres for ritual activity and the expression of religious beliefs. According to historical records, there were once several stone circles in Fife but only one example, that at Balbirnie (2), has survived into the present day.

The earliest known burial tradition in the region is represented by cist burials which date from around 2,500 BC onwards. Cists are small stone-lined graves usually measuring no more than one metre in length. The body was normally placed on its side in the cist with its knees drawn up to its chest. Often the burial was accompanied by a special type of pottery jar known as a Beaker. Occasionally other items such as a dagger or a jet necklace might be included within the grave. It has been suggested that the inclusion of pots and weapons within cists may indicate that our ancestors believed in an After-Life. This explanation may be borne out by the contents of a Beaker which was discovered in a cist burial at Ashgrove Farm near Methil (NT 352 999). Analysis of the pollen grains found within the Beaker showed that the pot contained mead made from lime honey and flavoured with the flowers of meadow-sweet. The sweet drink was perhaps intended as sustenance for the dead man on his journey to the After-World. (Both the Beaker and a dagger from this excavation may be seen at Kirkcaldy Museum).

Cist burials have been found both as isolated occurrences and in groups. The latter were often originally covered by great mounds of earth and stone known as barrows and cairns. Burial within these cists and cairns was a long-lived tradition which continued for over a thousand years, indeed for much of the period which archaeologists call the Bronze Age. This name derives from the discovery of bronze weapons and jewellery within the graves from around 2,000 BC onwards.

(i)   Cist Burial, Ashgrove Farm, Methil

Barrows and cairns were once common land-marks in the landscape of Fife. Digging into cairns was a popular pastime for gentlemen in the 19th century, however. As a result, many are known to us today only from descriptions in gentlemen's journals or early antiquarian publications. A few cairns do survive, often on hilltops or in conspicuous positions. Good examples may be seen at Collessie (NO 282 135) and Gateside (NO 195 090).

Burial within a stone-lined grave is only one of several funerary customs known to date from this period. Cremation was another common burial rite, the remains often being placed in a large pottery urn. As with cist burials, ciner-ary urns have been found both singly and in groups. Both traditions have also been found on the same site as in the example at Balbirnie stone circle and cairn.

Collessie Bell Cairn

Although Bronze Age burials are fairly common, the homesteads and farms of these first metalworkers are rare. A second group of monuments has survived from Bronze Age times, however. These are the standing stones, a common feature in the landscape of Fife. Standing stones occur either as single pillars, in pairs or in groups of four. Single stones are by far the most common occurrence but an example of paired stones may be seen at Glassmount, near Kinghorn (NT 243 883). Groups of four stones (sometimes called "four-posters") are known from historical records, but none has survived in Fife into the present day. The single standing stone visible at the roadside near Strathendry (NO 230 015) may perhaps be the sole survivor of one such group recorded in 1793.

Few standing stones have been excavated and their true purpose is uncertain. Several functions have been suggested for the stones, varying from boundary markers to burial memorials. The occasional discovery of cremation deposits or cist burials lying beneath the stones bears out the latter interpretation. Such burials have been found in Fife at Easter Pitcorthie (5) and Lundin Links (6).

(ii)   Cup-Marked Stone from Balbirnie Stone Circle

Some standing stones are decorated by carvings known as cup-markings. These carvings are formed by pecking out hollow depressions in the rock's surface and are sometimes surrounded by one or more rings. Cup-markings are known to have been used as a decorative art-form from 3,000 B.C. onwards. They are found, not only on standing stones, but also on cist slabs and boulders. Several stones in Fife have been decorated in this way, including the standing stones at Tuilyies (4) and Easter Pitcorthie (5). It could be that the carvings were originally intended to convey some meaning to our Bronze Age ancestors. Any such "message" has, unfortunately, been lost in the passage of time.

Forts, Villages and Farmsteads:
600 BC - AD 300

Towards the end of the Bronze Age considerable changes occurred. Weapons and tools initially made from bronze were gradually replaced by a new metal - iron. The types of weapons were changing too. In place of small daggers the warriors of the late Bronze Age and Iron Age carried spear and swords. This change in weapon types is mirrored in the archaeological remains. In marked contrast with earlier times, numerous fortified settlements are known to date from about 600 B.C. to AD 300. This emphasis on warfare and fortification is probably a reflection of a changing society. We know from a map of the world, produced in A.D. 140, that society in Scotland was organised into tribes. Each of those tribes occupied its own territory and conflict between neighbouring groups could well have been rife.

Many Iron Age settlements were located on hill tops or in upland areas where they have survived the erosive power of the plough. As a result they survive as earthen banks or tumbled stretches of walling which can still be seen today. Several different types of settlement are known to date from this period, varying from fortified villages to the individual homesteads of wealthy Celtic farmers.

The earliest known settlements are the fortified villages which were built on promontories or hilltop locations. Such hillforts were built throughout Britain at this time and there are several fine examples in Fife: East Lomond (7), Normans Law (9) and Saline Hill (NT 043 934). They are generally recognisable today from the ramparts and walls which protected their summits. Foundations of circular houses are occasionally visible within their interiors.

Although now ruinous and overgrown, the ramparts and walls of these forts were originally impressive defences against attack. This has been demonstrated by an excavation of the ramparts of Craigluscar fort (NT 059 909). This small fort was protected by three lines of defence; an inner stone wall, two high stockade fences and a second outer rampart to protect its most vulnerable flank.

The excellent defensive qualities of these hillforts ensured their use and re-use throughout several centuries.

Not all settlements were as large or as heavily defended as the hillforts, however. Isolated homesteads were also built during the last few centuries B.C. These were probably the homes of individual farming families. Generally a large round house made of timber was set within a yard and enclosed by an earthen bank and ditch. One such homestead in Fife was excavated at Scotstarvit (NO 360 109) and other similar sites have been found at Wemyss Hall Hill (NO 375 120) and Cowden Hill (NO 257 174).

(iv)   Saline Hill Fort

15

Larger, unprotected settlements with no enclosing walls have also been discovered using aerial photographs. These appear to have been small hamlets made up of several houses. They are occasionally associated with another class of structure - the souterrain - dating from the last few centuries B.C. and the first few centuries A.D. Souterrains are narrow underground passages built of stone and are usually set into well-drained slopes. They were probably used as store-houses for foodstuff such as grain. As they are not normally visible now at ground level, souterrains have generally been discovered accidentally. This was true in the example found at Kinloch (NO 279 115) which was discovered during ploughing in 1933. The site was only partially excavated before being covered over again. It is now visible only as a cropmark on aerial photographs, along with the settlement of which it formed a part.

A final Iron Age settlement type which requires consideration is the broch. These circular dry-stone towers, with hollow walls and internal galleries, are perhaps the most spectacular of Scottish ancient monuments. They date from the last few centuries B.C., and remained in use until at least 200 A.D. The general distribution of brochs is concentrated in the north and west of Scotland. A few outliers do occur, however, and one example is known from Fife. Brochs were probably built for well-to-do local families. To live in such an impressive stronghold would have brought not only security, but also considerable social status and prestige. The broch at Drumcarrow (13) is a humble specimen in comparison with its northern counterparts but is nonetheless well worth a visit.

The Roman Invasions

By the end of the 1st millennium B.C., a richly varied pattern of settlement was established in Fife. Some people lived in hill-top villages, others in isolated farms or in small unprotected hamlets. It was this diverse landscape which was encountered by the Roman army during the first centuries A.D.

The Roman army successfully invaded southern Britain in A.D. 43, and A.D. 79 saw the first of three military campaigns to be led against the northern tribes in an attempt to bring them under the authority of Rome.

Each successful campaign was followed by a period of settlement in Scotland. Forts were constructed and networks of military roads were established. However, little evidence of this Roman occupation has been found in Fife.

No major forts are known, but three temporary marching camps have been found. These camps, at Bonnytown (NO 546 127), Auchtermuchty (NO 242 118) and Edenwood (NO 357 116) are thought to date from the final military campaign. This was led by the Roman Emperor, Septimus Severus, between A.D. 208 and A.D. 211.

The periods of Roman occupation were mostly shortlived. Maintaining an army in hostile territory would have been a costly exercise, and Scotland, on the very fringes of the Empire, was of little material benefit to Rome. Each campaign was followed, therefore, by a gradual withdrawal of the army south of Hadrian's Wall. For much of the Roman period this wall formed the northern frontier of Rome's extensive Empire.

The Picts: AD 300 - 843

The presence of the powerful Roman army to the south of Hadrian's Wall must have posed a permanent threat to the security of the northern tribes. It was perhaps in response to this threat that the tribes united, towards the end of the 3rd century A.D., to form a single political unit, known as the Picts. The "Picti" or "Painted Ones" were first recorded in a Roman document in A.D. 297 and they remained an independent nation until the Picts and Scots united in A.D. 843.

Early historical documents make references to Pictish kings and battles. They also record the gradual conversion of the Picts to Christianity in the 6th and 7th centuries. Historical records are few, however, and mostly written by outsiders. Much of the knowledge of this period has therefore been derived from place-names and the archaeological remains.

A study of place names can provide a general picture of the extent of Pictish settlement in Fife. The most useful names are those which incorporate the Pictish word "pit", meaning a share or a piece of land. When combined with Gaelic words it produces names such as Pitlethie and Pitcorthie. Pitlethie was originally "Laithan's Share" and Pitcorthie means the "share with the standing stones". Three farms in Fife bear the name Pitcorthie and each has a standing stone in its vicinity.

Aside from the "pit" names little is known about Pictish settlement patterns, although a few Iron Age hillforts appear to have continued in use into Pictish times. The excavation of the fort at Clatchard Craig (NO 243 178), in advance of its destruction by quarrying, revealed at least two ramparts dating from the 6th to 8th centuries AD. Similarly the latest phases of fortification on Norman's Law (9) may also date from this time.

In archaeological terms the Picts are best known from their characteristic artwork. This is most commonly to be found on the carved symbol stones which occur throughout eastern Scotland to the north of the rivers Forth and Clyde. The general distribution of these stones reflects the territory of the Pictish Kingdom, with Fife marking its southern limit.

As with Bronze Age standing stones, many of the Pictish symbol stones were originally set upright in prominent locations. Pictish symbol stones can be easily distinguished from standing stones, however, by the elaborate symbols which have been carved on one or more of the stone's faces. Some of these symbols represent everyday objects such as mirrors and combs; others are representations of real or mythical animals. Many of the symbols are abstract designs, often based on geometric shapes. The latter are given descriptive names such as "Z-rods", "double-discs" and "notched rectangles". The significance of these symbols can only be guessed at but it has been suggested that they may represent family totems or emblems. Their widespread occurrence on upright stones implies that they were intended to be seen. They have, therefore, been variously interpreted as burial memorials, boundary markers or public proclamations of marriage alliances. However, the true nature of their message will probably always elude us.

Several symbol stones have been found in Fife. One stone, decorated with an incised figure of a bull, was found within the fort on the summit of East Lomond Hill. Other symbols have been carved on the walls of the Wemyss Caves (13) and in miniature on two silver plaques. These were found within a hoard at the foot of Norrie's Law (NO 409 073) and are held by the Royal Museum of Scotland, in Edinburgh.

With the establishment of Christianity during the 7th century, symbol stones gradually gave way to a new type of monument - the cross-slab. As with their predecessors, these slabs were designed to stand upright. Pictish symbols may still be found on the reverse face and side panels of some of these stones, but the dominant feature of the slabs was the Celtic cross. In time, Pictish symbols were replaced with new designs, depicting hunting scenes or stories from the Bible.

Several cross-slabs have been found in Fife, both complete and fragmentary. They may mark the site of Early Christian churches but unfortunately no trace of any structure remains. Two examples of complete cross-slabs may be seen in Crail (14) and at Largo Parish Church (15). Other fine examples of Early Christian sculpture are housed in the museum at St Andrews Cathedral (29).

Mediaeval Fife

The territory of the Pictish Kingdom lay on the east coast of Scotland to the north of the rivers Forth and Clyde. The lands to the south and west were occupied by other groups; Northumbrian Angles in the south-east, Britons in Strathclyde and Scots in Dalriada (Argyll). Conflict between these groups was common. In the middle of the 9th century, however, the Scots and Picts united under one king, Kenneth MacAlpin, and a single, unified

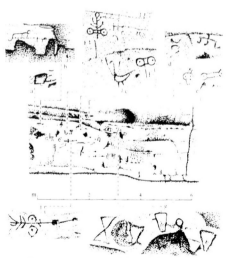

Wall Carvings, Court Cave, East Wemyss

19

nation emerged. The territories of Scotland were later enlarged in the early 11th century by the annexation of Strathclyde and in 1034 the Scottish border was extended southwards to the Tweed.

The centuries which followed saw many great changes; a feudal state was established, the church was re-organised and the first true towns were created. Much is known about this period from early historical documents but the widespread use of stone has also preserved many of the buildings which were erected at this time. The remains of these early buildings can help to reconstruct a picture of what mediaeval life must have been like. The structures which survive fall into three broad categories: fortified houses, churches and burghs.

Castles and Fortified Houses

In order to establish Scotland as a strong and secure state, the kings of the 11th and 12th centuries set about creating a feudal system of government. Under this system, the kings had absolute power and authority and were lords of all the land. They granted portions of land to their tenants-in-chief in exchange for loyalty and military service. The tenants-in-chief were also invested with some of the king's authority and were responsible for maintaining law and order within their lands. As landowners, they in turn were able to demand loyalty and services from their tenants.

In early mediaeval Scotland many of the tenants-in-chief were Anglo-Norman lords who were encouraged to move from their lands in England and to settle in Scotland. These incoming lords built timber castles which were set on top of artificial earth mounds known as mottes. The motte was protected by a high wooden fence or palisade and surrounded at its base by a ditch. The courtyard which surrounded the motte was known as a bailey and provided space for other buildings such as a chapel, stables and bakehouse.

These early timber castles provided a private residence for the feudal lord, his family and his retainers. They were also designed to be strongholds against attack. In time, however, the timber structures were replaced by stronger and more secure towers of stone. Although their wooden structures have long-since decayed and their ditches silted up, early mottes may still be seen today. They are recognisable as flat-topped grassy mounds and good examples may be seen at Leuchars (16) and at Maiden Castle, Kennoway (17).

In the 14th century mottes were replaced by tower-houses - a new style of building which was to dominate the landscape for some three hundred years. The basic plan of these structures consisted of a stone walled tower often set within a secure enclosure known as a barmkin. The tower contained all the basic accommodation required by the feudal lord and the enclosure provided space for ancillary buildings such as kitchens and stables.

Some of these towers were built on the site of the existing mottes, as in the example at Leuchars. Most occupied new sites, however, and their dominant position in the landscape mirrored the powerful status of their masters. The feudal lords were responsible for a good deal of local government and their castles were not only private residences but also centres for administration and justice.

Ballinbreich Castle

The need for defence was still strong in the 14th century and was met by the stout walls of the tower and its surrounding barmkin. Early towers also had few windows which gave them a closed-up, inward-looking quality. The ruinous towers of Ballinbreich (NO 271 204) and Balgonie Castle (19) are set within later courtyards which give a vivid impression of the defensive strength of these early stone castles.

The tower-house was an extremely successful building style and it remained the fashion throughout the 15th and 16th centuries. Gradually, however, the desire for comfort and amenity began to outweigh the need for strong defence. As a result the basic design was extended horizontally through the addition of one or more wings. Perhaps the best-preserved example of this building style in Fife is Scotstarvit (20) which dates from the early 17th century. This is a rather late example but it retains many of the design features of its earlier counterparts.

Kellie Castle

Castles and towers were not only built by feudal landlords but also by bishops and kings. The bishop's fortress at St Andrews (23) and the royal residence at Ravenscraig in Kirkcaldy (22) are perhaps two of the most impressive castles in Fife. As the need for strong defences decreased in the 16th century, however, so the design of royal residences changed from fortress to palace. These were designed to be comfortable and elegant homes, as can be seen from the two royal palaces in Fife; the classical Renaissance Palace at Falkland (24) and the converted Benedictine guest house in Dunfermline (NT 089 873).

The growing architectural trend towards style, elegance and comfort was gradually mirrored in the residences of the aristocracy. The wealthy landed gentry of the 17th and 18th centuries abandoned their cramped tower-houses in favour of new and grander styles of building. Some of the earlier towers continued in use but were expanded into magnificent homes. Excellent examples may be seen at Kellie Castle (NO 520 052) and Earlshall (NO 464 210). Most towers were abandoned, however, and left to fall into decay. Their numerous shell-like ruins may still be seen today and create a vivid reminder of times long past.

Early Churches

Along with the re-organisation of government in the 11th and 12th centuries a re-organisation of the church took place. Devout kings encouraged the building of many new churches and monasteries, the ruins of which may still be seen today.

For the first time the country was divided into parishes under the overall authority of a bishop. Each parish had its own church, usually built by the local feudal lord to meet the spiritual needs of his tenants. Most of these early churches were stone-built structures with a plain rectangular outline. Culross West Kirk (NS 980 865) is a good example of this. Internally, they were divided into two quite separate areas: a choir for the clergy in the east and a larger nave for the lay folk in the west. In the majority of churches this division was achieved by a wooden screen. Occasionally, however, the division was also created in stone. This type of plan may still be seen in two of Fife's oldest churches, the ruin of Parva Kinghorn in Burntisland (26) and the restored church of St Fillan's in Aberdour (27).

The bishop responsible for these parish churches had his seat in St Andrews. In contrast to the simplicity of the parishes, the bishop's church was designed on a very grand scale in order to reflect the importance of his role. The earliest known church to be built for the bishops of St Andrews was that of St Rule's which dates from the 11th century. This was eventually superceded in the later 12th century by the greatest of all Scottish mediaeval churches, St Andrews Cathedral (29).

In addition to the parish churches and cathedrals, many monasteries were also founded in the 12th and 13th centuries. Several European orders of monks established religious communities in Fife, the earliest being a Benedictine Abbey which was founded by Queen Margaret in Dunfermline (30). This was soon followed by other monastic communities - Augustinians at St Andrews, Tironensians at Lindores and Cistercian monks at Balmerino and Culross.

Culross Abbey

Many of these monasteries were founded by devout kings and lords who endowed the communities generously. They also gave them land. As a result, the monasteries became wealthy feudal land-owners in their own right. The great wealth of the mediaeval abbeys and priories can still be appreciated in the splendour of the churches which were built. Although many of Fife's monasteries are now in ruin, two examples clearly illustrate their original splendour. The magnificent nave of the abbey church at Dunfermline (30) is, without doubt, one of the finest examples of Scottish-Norman architecture, while the fine state of preservation of Inchcolm Abbey (31) conveys a particularly clear impression of mediaeval monastic life.

In addition to their existing wealth, many abbeys and priories were also able to draw upon the income of the parish churches. It was considered an act of piety for a land-owner to give the patronage of his parish church to a monastery. This meant that abbeys and priories gradually took over the running of parish affairs. Often, however, they kept much of the parish revenue for their own coffers and appointed a poorly paid vicar to see to the needs of the parishioners. This inequality of wealth between the abbeys and parish churches was nullified by the Reformation of the Church in the mid-16th century.

Following the Reformation, monasteries and cathedrals were abandoned and allowed to fall into decay. Some were even quarried for building stone. In the main the parish churches fared rather better because most parishes were too poor to contemplate new building. Once the fabric of these ancient churches began to fall into disrepair in the 18th and 19th centures, however, they were finally replaced by buildings of grander architectural pretensions. Many of the early parish churches were destroyed by the buildings which replaced them. Others survived, however, and, like the monasteries and cathedrals, stand as roofless ruins in the landscape.

Burghs

The early mediaeval churches and fortified houses were impressive buildings made of stone. In contrast, the houses of the ordinary farmers and land-owners were still made of wood and thatch and, unfortunately, no known trace of their homes survives. The same was true of the earliest buildings in the burghs but, fortunately, these were later replaced in stone.

The first burghs were created by royal charter in the early 12th century. Amongst the earliest to be established in Fife were Dunfermline (c.1124), Crail (c.1150) and Inverkeithing (c.1153). Burghs were simply secure towns enclosed by walls or palisade defences. The security which these towns offered soon attracted traders and craftsmen - weavers, tailors, bakers and masons.

The inhabitants of the royal burghs were given special privileges and they held exclusive rights to trade within the surrounding area. Country folk with produce to sell at the burgh fair were compelled to pay taxes on everything they sold and to accept the prices fixed by the burgh. Clearly there was profit to be made from being a burgh merchant. In return for these rights and privileges, the king demanded loyalty from the burgh. Royal burghs were also expected to pay taxes which were calculated according to their income from trade.

Not all burghs were created by the king. Many were burghs of barony which were established by the local feudal lord. These burghs had many of the privileges associated with royal burghs. The revenue from trade and tolls usually went to the local land-owner, however, rather than in taxes to the king. Some early burghs of barony, such as St Andrews, were established by a bishop rather than a lord.

Burghs were essentially, therefore, walled market towns. A few, such as Crail and Inverkeithing, had proper stone walls but this was expensive. As the walls were mainly intended to deter thieves and raiders, many burghs made do with enlarged garden walls. These formed a continuous barrier around the edge of the town, broken only by the burgh gates, known as yetts or ports. Most burgh walls and gates were taken down once their usefulness had passed. In many towns, however, the site of the gates can still be determined from names such as Port Street. One original gate still survives in Fife at the West Port in St Andrews (33).

Within the burgh walls the most imposing landmark was often a castle, abbey or palace. This was certainly true in the case of Falkland and St Andrews. In terms of its importance in everyday life, however, the most significant building within the burgh was the tolbooth. This building had several important functions. It was the place where the burgh council met, where market dues and taxes were paid, where burgh records were stored and where

Mercat Cross, Crail

prisoners were held. Many tolbooths survive in Fife, most dating from the 16th century onwards, e.g. Dysart (34), West Wemyss (35) and Crail (NO 613 077).

Tolbooths usually stood on the main street of the burgh at the point where it widened out to accommodate the market. Another common feature on the market place was the mercat cross. This was the symbol of the burgh's authority and became a focus for public gatherings. A great many mercat crosses can still be seen today but few are shaped like a cross. Most are stone pillars mounted on steps, which are often crowned by a unicorn or lion. Good examples of this type of "cross" may be seen at Crail (NO 613 078) and Inverkeithing (36).

Markets were often held on a weekly basis. This allowed merchants and craftsmen who did not own shops to set up stalls and sell their produce. Everday items such as fish, meat, wool and skins were readily available. Other goods such as iron, luxury textiles, wine and spices had to be imported from overseas. The importance of trade with Scandinavia, France and the Low Countries led to the development of trading ports in the royal burghs, particulary those on the east coast. The harbours were generally simple structures and often consisted of no more than a couple of wooden jetties. The stone-built harbour at Crail (37) however, may date from as early as the 16th century.

Numerous burghs along the east coast of Fife flourished as a result of overseas trade. The merchants who imported luxury goods for sale to the gentry grew rich and powerful. Many owned their own ships, and their wealth may still be appreciated today in the grand houses which they built. Many merchants' houses were built overlooking the shore, where ship-owners could watch for the arrival of their cargoes. Examples of such houses may be seen at the Sailor's Walk, Kirkcaldy, and the Gyles at Pittenweem.

Pan Ha', Dysart

The houses of poorer people were never as well built as those of the rich. It is perhaps not surprising, therefore, that they have not survived as well. However, many fine townhouses dating from the 17th and 18th centuries survive. Almost every burgh in Fife can boast examples of such houses, but those of Culross, Crail and the Pan Ha' in Dysart are particularly fine. These picturesque houses with their crow-stepped gables and pan-tiled roofs, together with the tolbooths and market crosses, the market places and the narrow closes and vennels, all help to create a vivid impression of what life in these early mediaeval burghs must have been like.

Part Two

A Gazeteer of Archaeological Sites

Symbols Used:

A property in the care of the Secretary of State for Scotland

A property owned by the National Trust for Scotland

A property covered by the Fife Ranger Service

Disabled Access

A Gazeteer of Archaeological Sites

1. Balfarg Henge
2. Balbirnie Stone Circle and Cairn
3. Harelaw Cairn
4. Tuilyies Standing Stone
5. Easter Pitcorthie Standing Stone
6. Lundin Links Standing Stones
7. East Lomond Fort
8. Maiden Castle Fort
9. Norman's Law Fort
10. Drumcarrow Broch
11. Abdie Old Kirk & Symbol Stone
12. Strathmiglo Symbol Stone
13. Wemyss Caves
14. Standing Stone of Sauchope
15. Largo Cross
16. Leuchars Castle
17. Maiden Castle
18. Aberdour Castle
19. Balgonie Castle
20. Scotstarvit Tower

21. Tulliallan Castle

22. Ravenscraig Castle

23. St Andrews Castle

24. Falkland Palace

25. Darisie Castle

26. Parva Kinghorn

27. St Fillan's Church, Aberdour

28. Leuchars Church

29. St Rule's Church &
    St Andrews Cathedral

30. Dunfermline Abbey

31. Inchcolm Abbey

32. Tulliallan Old Kirk

33. West Port, St Andrews

34. Dysart Tolbooth

35. West Wemyss Tolbooth

36. Inverkeithing Mercat
    Cross & Tolbooth

37. Crail Harbour

38. Culross Palace

1. Balfarg Henge

Excavations in 1977 and 1978 revealed that *Balfarg Henge* was used over a long period. It was first constructed around 2900 BC and remained in use for some 1500 years. In form it consisted of a level platform, 60 metres in diameter. This was enclosed within a circular ditch with an earthern bank on its outer edge. Within the interior of the henge a circle of sixteen massive timber posts was set upright. Two unusally large posts formed a detached porch or entrance on the west. This timber circle was later succeeded by two rings of standing stones. The final use of the site was marked by the slab-covered burial pit located close to the centre of the monument. This contained the burial of a young adult accompanied by a flint knife and a handled Beaker.

Following the excavation of the site the henge was partially reconstructed. Today the visitor will find that the ditch has been re-cut. A circle of sixteen short wooden posts indicating the location of the timber circle has also been set upright and the two surviving standing stones have been re-erected in their original positions.

How to get there:
O.S. Sheet 59 NO 281031
Balfarg Henge is now an area of open space within housing in Balfarg precinct, which lies in the northern area of Glenrothes New Town. Car parking is available on the roadside near to the site.

2. Balbirnie Stone Circle

The small *stone circle* at *Balbirnie* was excavated in 1970 and 1971 and in advance of a road widening scheme. The original circle measured 15 metres in diameter and consisted of 10 standing stones with a low rectangular setting at its centre. This Neolithic circle was later re-used as a Bronze Age burial site and several cists (stone-lined graves) were inserted within the boundary of the standing stones. One of the slabs which was used to line the graves was decorated with cup-markings and cup-and-ring markings. The final phase of activity at Balbirnie involved the sealing of the stone circle and the cist burials beneath a cairn of stones. At least sixteen cremation burials were contained within the cairn.

The main features of the site have been reconstructed in Balbirnie Park by Glenrothes Development Corporation. Eight of the ten original standing stones of the circle may still be seen and some of the cist burials have been reconstructed. A cast of one of the cup-marked stones has been included in this reconstruction, the original stone being held in the collection of the National Museum of Scotland.

How to get there:
O.S. Sheet 59 NT 285029
Balbirnie Park lies to the east of the A92 Glenrothes - Cupar road. Vehicle access to the park is from the B9130 Glenrothes - Markinch road. Car parking is available within the park.

3. Harelaw Cairn

Harelaw Cairn is a good example of a Bronze Age burial mound. Set close to the summit of Hare Law, it occupies a commanding position with a fine view overlooking the valley of the River Ore. The cairn measures some 29 metres in diameter and is over 3 metres high. An investigation was carried out in the 1890's and three cist burials were discovered. Two of these contained food vessels and the third produced a remnant of a bronze dagger. The broad trench which was cut through the cairn is still visible today, but the finds from the excavations have, unfortunately, been lost.

How to get there:
O.S. Sheet 58 NT 187961
Harelaw Cairn is situated to the east of the village of Crosshill, in Dunfermline District. The B920 Lochgelly - Scotlandwell Road runs through Crosshill. Access to the cairn is from Loanhead Avenue, Lochore, which runs east from the B920. From the end of Loanhead Avenue, access is via a track and a path leading to the cairn.

4. Tuilyies Standing Stone

Tuilyies is a fine example of a *cup-marked standing stone.* The grey sandstone pillar stands to a height of 2.4 metres and is decorated on its eastern face with numerous small cup-marks. The deep perpendicular grooves are not man-made, however, but the result of natural weathering. Three smaller boulders to the south of the standing stone are set in the form of a triangle and may also have formed part of this Bronze Age sacred site.

How to get there:
O.S. Sheet 65 NT029865
The standing stone is in a field on the south side of the A985, 1.5km west of the roundabout at Cairneyhill. The stone is visible from a layby on the roadside. Access to the field is forbidden. Cars may be parked on the layby.

5. Easter Pitcorthie Standing Stone

Easter Pitcorthie standing stone is a massive upright slab of red sandstone. It measures over 2.4 metres in height and some 3 metres in girth at its base. The southern face of the stone has been decorated with 33 cup-marks and two "dumb-bell" shaped carvings are also visible. Investigations by the farmer in the winter of 1852-3 revealed that a cremation deposit had been placed beneath the stone.

How to get there:
O.S. Sheet 59 NO 497039
The standing stone is located at Easter Pitcorthie Farm, approximately one mile east of Colinsburgh on the B942 Largo - Pittenweem road. The farm is on the north side of the road, and the standing stone is in the middle of a field to the west of the farm buildings. There is no organised car parking, and care must be taken not to obstruct farm vehicles. Permission to view the stone at close quarters should be sought from the farm.

6. Lundin Links Standing Stone

The three stone pillars at *Lundin Links* form the most impressive group of *standing stones* in Fife. Hewn from red sandstone, the irregularly-shaped blocks stand to heights of about 4.1, 4.6 and 5.5 metres. Although only three stones survive, a fourth is known to have existed towards the close of the 18th century. A stone-lined grave was also discovered near the stones in 1844.

How to get there:
O.S. Sheet 59 NO 404027
The Lundin Links standing stones are situated on one of the fairways of the Lundin Links Ladies Golf Club in Lundin Links. The Golf Club lies to the north of the A915 Leven - Largo road in the town of Lundin Links. Cars may be parked at the clubhouse, and the stones are about 700m west of the clubhouse.

7. East Lomond Fort

The summit of *East Lomond Hill* is occupied by a large and important Iron Age *fort.* At a height of 424 metres above sea level, the fort commands an impressive view. On a good day you can see right across the Howe of Fife and over the Firth of Tay to Dundee. Originally the flat-topped summit would have supported a small Iron Age community. Today all that survives are the protective ramparts and ditches.

The innermost wall of the fort is still clearly visible. It encircles the summit of the hill and forms a pear-shaped enclosure. No traces of any domestic structures remain within the interior. A large burial cairn has survived, however, and is now used as a view-point. The steep slopes around the inner enclosure still bear the traces of several additional ramparts and terraces. These are particularly well-preserved on the north east side of the hill. A further line of defence is also visible on the southern side of the fort. This was the easiest line of approach to the settlement and was protected by a massive bank and ditch.

How to get there:
O.S. Sheet 59 NO 244062
Midway between Falkland and the New Inn roundabout there is a minor road on the south side of the A912. The road is signposted to the car park on East Lomond from the car park on East Lomond. From the car park there is a well defined footpath to the summit of East Lomond.

8. Maiden Castle Fort

Maiden Castle is a small, isolated *fort.* It is set amidst rough ground between two low spurs of the Lomond Hills. Originally protected by marshland, the fort occupies a low, grassy knoll. This knoll must once have been the focus for a small defended settlement.

The best preserved feature of the site is a single earthen rampart with a ditch on its inner edge. This rampart runs around the base of the hillock on its north and south sides. Both the rampart and ditch die out at the western end of the hillock at what may once have been an entrance. The principal gate-way, however, was at the eastern end of the fort. Here there is a gap in the bank and ditch, some six metres wide.

How to get there:
O.S. Sheet NO 222068
Cars may be parked at Craigmead Car Park, on the minor road from Leslie to Falkland. Access to Maiden Castle is then by foot, along a well defined track, signed to West Lomond. The castle lies to the north of the track, north west of a small plantation.

9. Norman's Law

Norman's Law is the highest summit in a range of hills which overlooks the southern shore of the Tay. With magnificent views in all directions, this rocky hilltop was an ideal location for a *defended prehistoric settlement.* Traces of two such periods of fortification are visible around the summit. The later of these may have been a Pictish stronghold.

The walls of the earlier settlement encircle the whole of the summit area, with an outer line of defence protecting the terraces to the south. The later fortification is much smaller and occupies only the summit. Its stout walls are still well-preserved and are up to 5 metres thick. Traces of many domestic structures are also visible on the summit and lower terraces. These are known as "hut circles" and consist of the stone foundations of circular timber houses.

How to get there:
O.S. Sheet 59 NO 305201
Norman's Law is located approximately 5 miles north east of Newburgh. Access is possible from minor roads on the north side of the hill.

Two miles north of the crossroads between the A913 (Cupar - Newburgh) and the A914 (Glenrothes - Dundee) take the minor road North through Luthrie village and on towards Brunton village. Before reaching Brunton, follow the road to the left towards Newburgh. After passing Pittachope Farm on the right, find somewhere to park. Normans Law is on the left hand side of the road. Follow the footpath and field boundaries to summits.

As there is no organised parking, care must be taken not to obstruct farm vehicles or traffic using the road.

10. Drumcarrow Broch

Drumcarrow Broch is situated on top of a rock ridge known as Drumcarrow Craig, at a height of 217 metres above sea-level. It was once the site of a strong and impressive tower which dominated the landscape and commanded excellent views over the surrounding countryside. Today the Iron Age tower is sadly tumbled and ruinous, and a modern cairn overlies its western wall.

The broch is circular in outline and measures approximately 14 metres in diameter with a wall some 5 metres thick. The outer face of the wall is traceable for the greater part of its circuit and a few inner facing stones are visible in places. No internal features have survived but the entrance passageway may still be seen on the eastern side of the tower. This is now choked with rubble, as is the broch's interior.

How to get there:
O.S. Sheet 59 NO 459132
Drumcarrow Craig is situated about three miles south of Strathkinness village, within the triangle formed by the B939, A915 and B940. From the minor road between Peat Inn and Strathkinness, take the road to Drumcarrow Farm. The access to the broch is opposite Drumcarrow Farm. There is no organised parking and care should be taken not to obstruct the road or farm vehicles.

The remains of the broch are between the triangulation point and the cairn at the top of the hill. The gates on the track should be kept closed, and dogs must be kept under control.

11. Abdie Old Kirk & Symbol Stone

At the entrance to *Abdie Old Churchyard* is a small building which houses a *carved symbol stone*. This stone originally stood on a low hill overlooking the village of Lindores. Over the years it has served several functions. Most recently it has been re-used as a sundial and as an Ordnance Survey bench mark. The original use of the stone, however, was as a Pictish symbol stone.

The Pictish symbols are well-carved and are still clearly visible. Two of the carvings may be seen on the front face of the stone. The upper design is known as a triple disc symbol and is thought to represent a cauldron. The lower design is a crescent and V-rod symbol. The V-shaped rod is interpreted as a broken arrow. A third design, the mirror symbol, is carved on one side of the stone.

Within the churchyard are the ruins of Abdie Old Kirk. This is a fine example of an early parish church which dates from the 13th century. It was originally a simple structure consisting of a single chamber. An aisle was added on the north in the 17th century, however. The belfry and south porch also date from this time. The church continued in use until 1827 when it was abandoned in favour of the new building, some 500 metres to the north.

How to get there:
O.S. Sheet 59 NO 259163
From the minor road between Lindores (three miles south of Newburgh) and Grange of Lindores, take the road immediately west of the railway bridge. Continue past the parish church to Abdie Cottage and Abdie Old Kirk. There is no formal parking, and care should be taken not to block the road.

12. Strathmiglo Symbol Stone

The *Strathmiglo symbol stone* had been used as a gate-post for many years before its "discovery" in the late 1960's. It has now been re-erected outside the churchyard wall. The tall pillar of stone stands to a height of some 1.7 metres and is decorated by two Pictish carvings. Although heavily weathered, the two symbols may still be clearly seen. One of the carvings is a representation of a hind's head while the other is a geometric design, known as the "tuning-fork" symbol.

How to get there:
O.S. Sheet 58 NO 216102
Strathmiglo village is located three miles west of Auchtermuchty, just off the A91. The church is at the eastern end of the village. Cars may be parked beside the church. The symbol stone is just outside the churchyard, next to the entrance.

13. Wemyss Caves

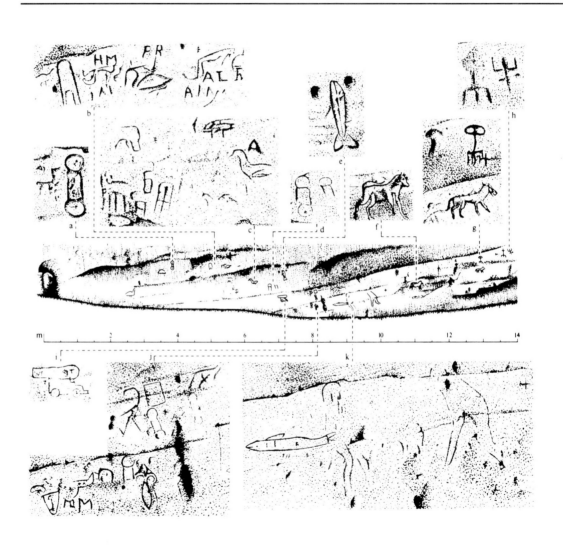

The name Wemyss derives from the Gaelic word "uamh", meaning a *cave*. There were originally 12 coastal caves along the shore at Wemyss, six of which may still be visited today. Pictish symbols are carved into the walls of four of the caves. These carvings have been studied for over 100 years and the first careful drawings were made in the mid-nineteenth century. Unfortunately, several of the symbols which were visible at that time have since been destroyed.

The most westerly of the caves is known as the Court Cave. This is a twin entranced cave which is now supported by pillars. The clearest carving in the main cavern is the "sceptre" which is flanked by a "double-disc" symbol. Another double disc symbol may be seen on a higher ledge. A third carving is also clearly visible in the small opening at the entrance to main cave. This represents an animal accompanied by a human figure, brandishing a spear.

Further along the shore is the Doo Cave. This gets its name from the pigeon nests which have been hewn out of the rock. The nests may still be seen but a rock fall from the roof has closed off the rest of the cave. This collapse destroyed the symbols which were once carved on its walls.

No ancient carvings have been found in the Well Caves, below MacDuff's Castle. Further along the shore, however, is Jonathon's cave - a large cavern with Pictish symbols carved out on both walls. Several of these carvings are quite well preserved. They include double disc symbols, an oared ship and naturalistic animals such as a fish and a horse.

The most easterly of the caves is the Sliding Cave which gets its name from its sloping floor. This falls away steeply from the narrow entrance and the cave should be entered with care. Three carvings may be seen on the walls. Two are rectangular markings and the third is a double disc symbol.

How to get there:
O.S. Sheet 59 NO 340970
The Wemyss Caves lie on the shoreline at East Wemyss. East Wemyss lies on the A955 Kirkcaldy - Leven road. From the A955 follow the signs to "The Shore". Cars may be parked at the shore, and it is possible to walk along the shore to the Caves. Jonathon's Cave is now protected by a locked gate. Permission to enter should be sought from the Wemyss Environmental Centre at East Wemyss Primary School, on the main road.

14. Standing Stone of Sauchope

The *Standing Stone of Sauchope* is an Early Christian *cross-slab* which probably dates from the 9th century. It originally stood on a small mound near the farm of Sauchope but was moved to its present position in Crail Church in 1929. The slab bears a carved Celtic cross on one side and traces of sculpture on the other. The cross is still clearly visible but unfortunately the stone is heavily weathered and the sculptures are now almost indecipherable.

How to get there:
O.S. Sheet 59 NO 610078
The stone is located not far from the centre of Crail. Leaving Crail on the A917 towards St Andrews the stone is situated in Victoria Gardens, on the west side of the road. Car parking is available in the Marketgate, next to the Town House at the north end of the High Street. The stone can be seen from the roadside.

15. Largo Cross

Largo Cross is an Early Christian *cross-slab* which is decorated with both Pictish and Christian symbols. It was discovered in 1839 on the Largo Estate and was initially set up in the grounds of Largo House. On the sale of the estate it was moved to Arniston in Midlothian. It was eventually returned, however, and was placed in its present position in the gateway of the parish church.

The dominant feature of the slab is the carved Celtic cross. This is carved in relief and was originally decorated with interlace. Unfortunately, the stone is heavily weathered and the intricate decoration is only visible in places. Aside from the cross, the front panel also bears two sea-horses twisted together. The reverse face of the cross is decorated with a hunting scene showing three horsemen accompanied by dogs.   Below this are two animals, resembling deer, and a characteristic Pictish carving, known as the "elephant" symbol.

How to get there:
O. S. Sheet 59 NO 423034
Upper Largo village (also known as Kirkton of Largo) is located approximately10 km east of Leven, where the A915 meets the A917. Taking the minor road on the north side, next to the garage, follow the road round into Church Place. Car parking is available on the road near to the church. The cross-slab is situated just inside the church gate, within a protective iron fence.

16. Leuchars Castle

Leuchars Castle motte is the site of an early mediaeval tower. It was originally built of wood but later replaced in stone. The original timber castle was probably built in the 12th century by one of the Norman lords, who were given lands in Scotland by King David I.

The site now consists of an oval, flat-topped mound, some 80 metres long by 50 metres wide and 8 metres high. This mound is an artificial construction and was originally surrounded by a moat. No trace remains of the first timber tower and the stone castle which succeeded it was demolished in the 18th century. The site has never been excavated but an engraved bronze plate was found near the mound in 1923. This dates from the 13th century and is decorated with figures dressed in the typical costume of that time. The plate is held in the Royal Museum of Scotland in Edinburgh.

How to get there:
O. S. Sheet 59 NO 454219
Leuchars Castle is located to the north of Leuchars village in the middle of a field adjacent to the disused railway line. Car parking is available in Leuchars village. From the roundabout joining the Main Street (A919) and Station Road, walk north from the Commercial Arms Hotel along the disused railway line. The Motte can be viewed from the locked gates.

17. Maiden Castle, Kennoway

Maiden Castle, Kennoway is the site of an early mediaeval *motte.* It is traditionally associated with Macduff, Thane of Fife who lived in the second half of the 11th century and who was immortalised in Shakespeare's play, "Macbeth".

Today the site is a steep man-made hill with a circular flat-topped summit. This summit measures some 21 metres in diameter and would originally have been crowned by a timber castle. It would also have been protected by a high palisade fence and surrounded at its base by a moat. Unfortunately no trace of any structure survives.

How to get there:
O.S. Sheet 59 NO349015
Maiden Castle, Kennoway, is situated to the east of the main A916 Windygates - Cupar road, behind the Burns Tavern, to the south of Kennoway. Cars may be parked at the roadside, and the motte is easily visible from the road.

18. Aberdour Castle

Aberdour Castle is one of the oldest stone castles in Fife. It was first mentioned in historical documents in about 1325. In that year the barony of Aberdour was granted to the Earl of Moray by his uncle, King Robert the Bruce. In 1342 the Earl of Moray then granted a charter of the barony to his friend, Sir William Douglas. The castle has remained in the possession of the Douglas family ever since.

The oldest part of the castle is the western tower. This was originally a free-standing tower-house built in the 13th century. It is now sadly ruinous and only the basement and south-east wall survive. Over the years the accommodation provided by this tower proved insufficient for the earl and his household. A new range was therefore added in the 16th century, linked to the original tower by means of a turnpike stair. The new building contained a kitchen and store on the ground floor with more spacious living accommodation on the two floors above. In the 17th century a further L-shaped range was added on the east. Although the rest of the castle is ruinous, part of the eastern range is still in use today.

To the south, the castle looks out over garden terraces, beyond which stands a fine example of a 16th century dovecot. This was built in the shape of a bee-hive and contains 600 nests. To the east of the castle grounds is the ancient church of St Fillan's. (See No. 27)

How to get there:
O.S. Sheet 66 NT 192854
Aberdour Castle is situated near Aberdour railway station, which is on the main A92 Forth Road Bridge - Burntisland Road. Car parking is available at the station, and the entrance to the castle is adjacent to the entrance to the station car park.

19. Balgonie Castle

Balgonie Castle is a fine example of a mediaeval *tower-house* set within a courtyard enclosure. It is first mentioned in the late 14th century when the lands belonged to a family named Sibbald. In 1491 the property came by marriage to Sir Robert Lundie and the "tower-fortalice and manor" remained in his family until the early 17th century. The estate was then acquired by Major-General Sir Alexander Leslie. He was later created Lord Balgonie and became the first Earl of Leven. In 1824 the castle passed to the Balfour family, and later the Balgonie Estate. In 1971 the castle was purchased by Mr David Maxwell, who carried out considerable restoration work to the tower. In 1985 the castle was sold to the present owners, the family of Morris of Eddergoll, now styled Morris of Balgonie and Eddergoll, who are continuing to restore the castle.

The oldest part of the castle is the tower-house which dates back to the early 15th century. The four-storey tower is well-preserved and has been little altered over the years. Each floor consists of a single chamber. The ground floor probably served as a store-house, while a hall and private chambers would have occupied the rooms above. These four floors combined would have provided all the basic accommodation required by the earliest lords of Balgonie. Over the years, however, additional ranges were built around the courtyard. These were designed to provide more comfortable living quarters than the cramped rooms of the tower. The north range was probably built by Sir Robert Lundie in 1496. It consisted of a kitchen on the ground floor with a hall and chamber above. The ruinous ranges are the youngest part of the castle, having been built in the 17th century by the first Earl of Leven.

How to get there:
O.S. Sheet 58 NO 312006
Balgonie Castle lies on the south bank of the River Leven, just south of the A911 Glenrothes Windygates road. From the A911 take the minor road south signed to Milton of Balgonie. Continue south through the village, across the River Leven and follow the the road as it turns west. Balgonie Castle is on the right, about 0.5 km further on.

20. Scotstarvit Tower

Scotstarvit Tower is thought to have been built by Sir John Scot in the early 17th century when he acquired the lands of "Tarvett" from Alexander Inglis. In 1612 his lands in Fife were incorporated as the barony of Scotstarvit. An older tower on the barony of Tarvit is mentioned in a charter in 1579. This was probably replaced by the present building in 1627. The present tower is in an excellent state of preservation and is perhaps the finest example of a ***tower-house*** in Fife. Note the small size of the windows and the closed up, inward-looking quality which is typical of these mediaeval houses.

The tower is L-shaped in plan and is five storeys and a garret in height. The smaller of the two wings houses a turnspike stair. This is continous from ground level to parapet and is capped by a conical spire. A door at the stair-head opens out onto the parapet walk and an armorial panel may be seen above the door. The panel bears the initials of Sir John and his first wife, Dame Anne Drummond, along with the date 1627. The larger wing of the tower comprises five main floors. Each of these consists of a single chamber, with the exception of the second floor which is divided into two separate rooms. None of the rooms was used as a kitchen.

This was probably housed in an outbuilding in order to minimise the risk of fire.

How to get there:
O.S. Sheet 59 NO 370112
Scotstarvit Tower is located just off the A912 between Cupar and Craigrothie, opposite Hill of Tarvit Mansion House. Scotstarvit Tower is in the care of the Secretary of State for Scotland, but the keys are held at Hill of Tarvit, which is owned by the National Trust for Scotland. Car parking is available at either Hill of Tarvit, or at the side of the A916, where there is space to pull off. A track leads from the main road to Scotstarvit Tower.

21. Tulliallan Castle

A few noblemen in the 14th century chose not to build tower-houses, but instead favoured a less forbidding form of dwelling - the *hall-house.* This consisted of a timber-roofed hall set over a vaulted undercroft. Although ruinous, *Tulliallan Castle* is one of the best preserved examples of this building style in Scotland.

The castle was originally a simple rectangular building. The two wings which project from the northern wall were added at a later date. The ground floor is divided into two vaulted chambers, the easternmost of which was apparently the original Hall. Two turnpike stairs in the western wall give access to the first floor which is similarly divided into two separate rooms. The upper floors are now inaccessible.

The hall-house was built as a stronghold against attack and an interesting feature at Tulliallan is the design of the principal entrance. This is in the south-west tower and was originally protected by a barred door, portcullis and drawbridge. The drawbridge no longer exists but the narrow vertical opening for its chain may be seen above the doorway. The entrance was also set back slightly into the wall in order to receive the drawbridge when raised.

How to get there:
O.S. Sheet 65 NS 926887
Tulliallan Castle is situated on the north west side of Kincardine, west of the A977 Kincardine - Alloa road, about 700m from the centre of the town. Car parking is available in the centre of Kincardine. Access to the castle is by foot along Fere Gait (the A977) to a track just before a row of houses known as Castlepark. The track crosses the railway, and then forks. The right fork, leading through the woods, gives access to the castle.

22. Ravenscraig Castle

Ravenscraig is one of the most impressive *castles* in Fife. It stands on a rocky promontory jutting out into Kirkcaldy Bay. This naturally defensive position is further enhanced by a deep rock-cut ditch. The castle was built by King James II for his queen, Mary of Gueldres. Work began in 1460 and continued until the queen's death in 1463. Seven years later James III granted the castle to William, Lord Sinclair, in partial exchange for the castle of Kirkwall and the earldom of Orkney.

In plan the castle consists of two round towers linked by a central range. The main entrance is in the middle of the central block and is reached by a permanent bridge spanning the ditch. The barrel-vaulted passageway opens out onto a natural courtyard, formed by the enclosed promontory. From here two stairways give access to the main living quarters in the towers. The kitchens and offices were located in the fragmentary buildings on the eastern side of the promontory. The castle was one of the first in Scotland to be designed to withstand artillery. Notable features are the embrasures for small guns in the upper part of the central block and the massively thick walls of the twin towers.

How to get there:
O.S. Sheet 59 NT290924
Ravenscraig Castle is located at Pathhead, to the east of Kirkcaldy Harbour, at the junction of the A921 (St. Clair Street) and the A955 (Nether Street). Car parking is available in the nearby Ravenscraig Park, off Dysart Road.

23. St Andrews Castle

St Andrews Castle was originally built in about the year 1200 as the palace and fortress residence of the bishops and later archbishops of St Andrews. It was destroyed and rebuilt on several occasions throughout its history. The surviving ruins date from the 16th century but they overlie and incorporate the remains of several earlier structures.

The castle buildings are set around the impressive courtyard which occupies an easily defended position. It is bordered by sea-cliffs on the north and east and by a rock-cut ditch on the south. To enter the courtyard pass across a bridge and through a vaulted pend. Above the pend is a range of ruinous buildings. These originally served as living quarters and gave access to the four-storey Fore Tower. The fragmentary buildings to the east of the Fore Tower are all that remains of the chapel range. The eastern range of buildings probably contained the dining hall but this has been completely destroyed by the erosive power of the sea.

On the northern side of the castle courtyard are the remains of two towers. The Kitchen Tower in the northeast corner of the courtyard consists of two vaulted cellars beneath a ruinous kitchen. The Sea Tower stands in the northwest angle and houses the castle prison.

One of the ground floor rooms of this tower is a dark and windowless chamber with a deep rock-cut pit beneath its floor, known as the "Bottle Dungeon".

A feature of the castle which is probably unique is the rock-cut siegeworks - a mine and countermine - which were tunnelled beneath the castle during a siege from 1546-7. Both the mine and countermine are today lit by electricity and may be visited in safety.

How to get there:
O.S. Sheet 59 NO 512169
St Andrews Castle is located at the north east side of St Andrews, at the end of the Scores. Car parking is available at a number of sites in the town.

24. Falkland Palace

The *Royal Palace* at *Falkland* is the focal point of the small burgh. It was built by the Stuart Kings between 1530 and 1541 and was used by them as a hunting lodge. The present building occupies the site of an earlier 15th century palace which in turn replaced a 13th century castle. The latter was destroyed by English invaders during the Wars of Independence in 1337. The excavated ruins of this 13th century building lie to the north of the present-day palace.

The elegant Renaissance palace of the Stuart Kings was built around a quadrangular court-yard. Of the original building only the south and east ranges survive. The latter is now ruinous but the south range was completely restored in the 19th century. To enter the palace courtyard pass through a pend beneath the impressive gate-tower. On either side of the gateway is a porter's lodge and the upper floors of this four-storey building served as the keeper's or captain's quarters.

Entrance to the well-preserved south range is gained via a turnpike stair in the south-east angle of the courtyard. The ground floor consists of 6 vaulted cellars, while the first floor has a series of habitable chambers opening off a gallery. On the upper floor is a chapel with a finely carved oak ceiling.

In contrast to the well-preserved south range, the eastern quarter is now roofless and ruinous. The ground floor of this three-storey block was originally a vaulted cellarage, whilst the first floor consisted of three large en-suite chambers. These are thought to have been the royal apartments. The arrangement of the upper floor is now uncertain.

Aside from the main palace building, a particularly interesting feature of Falkland is the Royal Tennis Court. This is attached to the stable block and lies to the north of the palace grounds. It was built for James V in 1539 and is still used regularly today.

The museum, which is housed in the palace, has an archaeological exhibition which includes a number of carved stones and Pictish symbol stones.

How to get there:
O.S. Sheet 59 NO253074
Falkland Palace is in the centre of Falkland, on the High Street. Car parking is available either on the High Street, or in the signposted car park.

25. Dairsie Castle

Dairsie Castle stands on high ground overlooking the River Eden about a mile south of Dairsie village. Dating from the 16th century, this ruined castle was once the home of John Spottiswood, Archbishop of St Andrews from 1615 to 1639. The parish church of St Mary's which stands some 50 metres to the east of the castle, was also built by Archbishop Spottiswood in 1621.

Dairsie Castle was originally a three storey building with towers projecting from its north and south angles. Today it is largely ruinous, but both the towers and fragments of the northwest and southeast walls are still fairly well-preserved. The basements of both towers are vaulted, as was the basement of the main block which served as a kitchen. The upper floors of the main block provided living accommodation, each floor being divided into two chambers. The north tower housed the stairway to the upper floors but the original function of the south tower is unknown. Its basement walls are pierced by gun loops and its upper floors were later converted into a dovecot when the castle went out of use.

How to get there:
OS sheet 59 NO 413160
Dairsie Village lies on the A91(T) Cupar - St. Andrews road. Approximately 1.5 km west of Dairsie, take the minor road to the south signed to "Dairsie Bridge (Ancient Monument)" Dairsie Castle lies to the north west of Dairsie Church between the railway line and the River Eden. Pedestrian access to the castle is via a footpath alongside the churchyard. There is no offical car parking and care should be taken not to cause an obstruction.

26. Parva Kingorn

Parva Kingorn ("Little Kinghorn") is an *old parish church* which dates from the early 13th century. It is said to have been dedicated to St. Serf and is known to have been consecrated by the bishop of St Andrews in the year 1243.

The church is a simple rectangular building which is now in a ruinous condition. In places the walls are fairly complete, but in others only the overgrown foundations survive. Of particular interest in this early church is the internal structural division into two distinct areas. The choir in the eastern half of the church was used by the clergy, while a large nave in the west was provided for the lay folk. A simple archway permitted movement between these two areas. This may still be seen but it was partially blocked at a later date when the choir was re-used as a burial place.

How to get there:
O.S. Sheet 66 NT230863
Despite its name, Parva Kingorn is the former parish church of Burntisland. It is situated on Church Street, in the northern part of Burntisland, known as "Kirkton". Church Street runs north from the A92 Aberdour Road, approximately 0.5km west of the roundabout where the A909, A92 and B923 meet. Cars may be parked on the roadside on Church Street.

27. St Fillan's Church

The *Old Parish Church of St Fillan's* in Aberdour is an ancient building which was established over 800 years ago. It is known to have been in existence by 1178 and it remained in regular use until 1796. In that year it was abandoned in favour of the new church at Wester Aberdour and it was allowed to fall into decay. For over a hundred years it stood roofless and ruinous but it was carefully restored in 1925. Today it is still in regular use as a place of public worship.

The restored church is the product of three periods of building, the oldest of which dates from the 12th century. In its earliest form the church was a simple rectangular building which was subdivided into a choir and nave. In the 16th century it was considerably altered, however, by the addition of the south aisle and entrance porch. The latest addition to the chuch was made in the 17th century when a low transeptal aisle was added on the north.

How to get there:
O.S. Sheet 66 NT193854
St Fillan's Church is just off the main road (the A921) running through Aberdour. The entrance to the church is to the east of the railway bridge, near Hawkcraig Road, which leads down to Silver Sands and Hawkcraig Point. Cars may be parked either at the station or at the car park at the bottom of Hawkcraig Road.

28. Leuchars Church

The *Parish Church* of *Leuchars* was originally built in late 12th century. It was first mentioned in a historical document in 1187 when it was recorded amongst the possessions of the priory of St Andrews. It was also known to have been dedicated to St Athernase by the Bishop of St Andrews in the year 1244.

Leuchars was particularly unusual amongst early parish churches for its elaborate design and rich external decoration. Over the years the church has been greatly altered, however, and the present building is a curious mixture of building styles. Only the choir of the original 12th century church survives today. This is elaborated at its eastern end by the provision of a curved apse - a vaulted structure which was designed to house the altar. The apse was originally roofed with timber but this was replaced in the 17th century by the bell turret which still adorns the church today. Particularly worthy of note are the external walls of the 12th century choir and apse. They are richly decorated with arcades and the wall-heads bear the carved images of oxen, rams, monsters and human grotesques.

<u>How to get there:</u>
O.S. Sheet 59 NO445213
Leuchars Village is located on the A919 between St Andrews and Newport-on-Tay. The church is situated on a prominent knoll in the centre of the village. A one-way system operates around the church. Parking is available behind the church.

St Rule's Church
29. & St Andrew's Cathedral

St Rule's is the earliest surviving *church* in Fife. It dates from the late 10th or early 11th century and was the first church to be built for the bishops of St Andrews. It was served by a group of Augustinian canons, brought to St Andrews by Bishop Robert in 1127. St Rule's remained in use over several centuries but was eventually succeeded by the grandest church ever built in Scotland - the cathedral church of St Andrews. Work was begun on the cathedral in 1160 and the completed building was finally consecrated in 1318 in the presence of King Robert the Bruce.

St Rule's Church now lies in ruins. The choir is roofless but the tall square tower has survived intact and stands to a height of 33 meters. The original church was much longer with a nave extending westwards from the tower. This part of the building would have been used by the lay folk but it has now completely disappeared. All that remains to prove its existence is a groove cut into the tower masonry which was designed to receive the edge of the roof.

St Andrews cathedral was built on a site adjacent to St Rule's. This magnificent church remained in use until the Reformation when it was abandoned and allowed to fall into decay. Unfortunately, much of the stone was used as a source of local building material and all that remains today are the east and west gables along with parts of the south wall. The cruciform outline of the original building has been marked out on the turf and the foundations of most of the supporting piers may also still be seen.

How to get there:
O.S. Sheet 59 NO513166
The cathedral is located at the east end of St Andrews town centre, where North Street and South Street meet, overlooking the sea. Car parking is available at a number of sites in the town.

30. Dunfermline Abbey

Dunfermline Abbey was one of the largest and most influential monasteries in Scotland. It was established in 1070 when the first Benedictine monks were brought to Dunfermline by Queen Margaret. The great monastic church was founded in 1128 by her son, David I, and was completed in 1250. During the Wars of Independence in the 13th century the monastery became a favourite rallying point for the Scottish barons. As a result, it was destroyed by Edward I in 1303. Only the church was spared. The monastic buildings were restored by King Robert the Bruce in the 14th century but were allowed to fall into decay after the Reformation.

Much of the ruinous monastery may still be appreciated today. Of the magnificent 12th century church only the nave has survived but it remains one of the finest examples of Scottish Norman architecture. The rest of the building was removed in 1819 to make way for the present parish church. In the course of rebuilding, workmen uncovered the grave of King Robert the Bruce. The remains were later reburied within the modern church and the memorial brass which covers the grave forms an interesting feature below the present pulpit.

To the south and east of the church is a graveyard. This occupies the site of the original cloister around which the monastic buildings were arranged. The fragmentary remains of the monk's dormitories maybe seen in the south east of the cloister area. To the west of these, running parallel with the church, is the refectory or dining hall. This was originally a three storey building of which the south wall and west gable survive. St Catherine's Wynd separates the refectory from the kitchens and guest house. Originally built in the 14th century, the guest house was substantially altered in the 16th century to create a royal palace. Communication between the palace and refectory was maintained via "The Pends", a well preserved gatehouse across St Catherine's Wynd.

How to get there:
O.S. Sheet 65 NO890873
The Abbey is in the centre of Dunfermline. Car parking is available at a number of sites in the town centre, and access to the Abbey is then best gained on foot.

31. Inchcolm Abbey

Inchcolm Abbey is thought to have been founded in about 1123 by King Alexander I. According to tradition, the king was caught in a storm while crossing the Firth of Forth at Queensferry. He was storm-bound on the island of Inchcolm for three days and was sheltered there by a hermit. In gratitude for his safety the king established a monastic settlement of Augustinian canons.

The *abbey* on *Inchcolm* is an extremely well-preserved example of a mediaeval monastic settlement. The fine state of preservation of the buildings is perhaps due to the island's isolated position. A partial demolition of the church did take place in 1581, however, in order to obtain building stone for a new tolbooth in Edinburgh. As a result of the demolition, the church is the most ruinous part of the abbey. In places no more than the foundations survive. A particularly rare and interesting feature of the church is a fragment of 13th century wall-painting which illustrates clerical figures outlined in black, red and yellow.

To the south of the ruinous church is the quadrangular cloister around which the living quarters are arranged. The buildings are two storeys in height. The lower storeys consisted of covered galleries while the upper floors provided living accommodation. On the ground floor the eastern galley gives access to the chapter house. This is an octagonal building which was used as the meeting place of the monastic community. The upper floor of the eastern range was used as the monks' dormitory. A night stair from the dormitory leads directly down into the church and another stair leads off to the warming house. This was the only room in the abbey in which the monks were permitted a fire to warm themselves.

To the south of the dormitory is the reredorter or latrine. The ruinous buildings which lie outwith the cloister to the east of the latrine are thought to have been used as the abbey's infirmary. Access to the south and west ranges fo the cloister is gained via a stairway in the south-west angle of the courtyard. The south range contained the kitchens and refectory while the west range was used as a guest house. The rooms in the north range of the cloister, above the 12th century church, are thought to have formed the abbot's private chambers.

How to get there:
O.S. Sheet 66 NT189826
The island of Inchcolm lies in the Firth of Forth, 2km south of Aberdour. A ferry operates from Aberdour harbour, weather permitting. The ferry is signed, in Aberdour, from the main A92 road.

32. Tulliallan Old Kirk

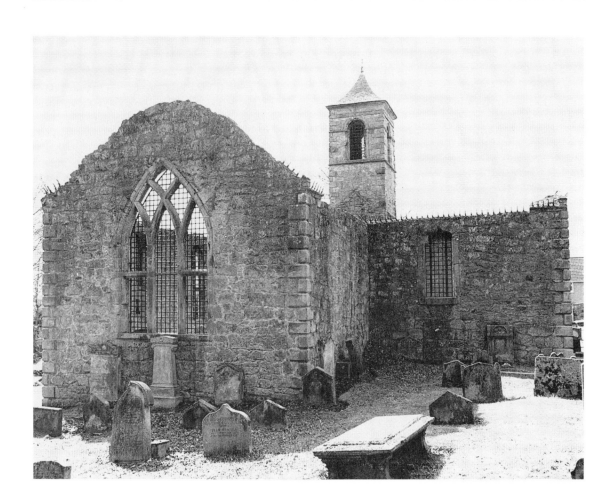

Tulliallan Old Kirk is a rare example of an early post-Reformation church in Fife. It was built in 1675 to replace an earlier mediaeval chapel but was itself superseded by the present parish church in 1833.

Today the old kirk still stands within its churchyard. Although roofless since the early 19th century, its walls are still fairly well-preserved. The basic outline of the building is rectangular with a transeptal aisle on the north. A square bell-tower stands at the west end and a panel above its doorway bears the date 1675 - the year of the church's foundation. Within the churchyard are many old tombstones which bear carvings of sailing ships. These reflect the sea-faring nature of the old parish community.

How to get there:
OS Sheet 65 NS 933880
The old kirk lies at the end of Kirk Street, Kincardine on Forth, beyond the present parish church. Cars may be parked at various locations in the centre, although on street parking is not encouraged, as Kincardine is the meeting place of three trunk roads, the A985(T), the A876(T) which crosses Kincardine Bridge, and the A777(T). Kirk Street runs north from the roundabout in the centre of Kincardine.

33. West Port, St Andrews

The **West Port,** standing at the west end of South Street in *St Andrews,* is one of the few surviving examples of a burgh gate in Scotland. It was erected in 1589 and the original building still survives. The contract was between master David Russell, Dean of Guild, and Thomas Robertson, a mason from Blebo.

The port consists of a central archway, some 3.5 metres wide, set between two semi-octagonal turrets. The smaller archways on either side are of modern construction and were probably added when the port was renovated in 1843. The carved panel above the central archway is also a modern addition. It replaced an original panel which bore the burgh coat of arms.

How to get there:
O.S. Sheet 59 NO505165
The West Port is located near St Andrews town centre on the west end of South Street where the A91 meets the A915 and the B939. Car parking is available at a number of sites in the town.

34. Dysart Tolbooth

Dysart became a burgh of barony in 1549 and many of the picturesque houses of this little coastal town date from the late 16th and early 17th centuries. The burgh *tolbooth* was erected in 1576 and was enlarged to accommodate a prison in the early 17th century.

The original tolbooth building is a roughly square tower-house with a stair-turret projecting from its north-east angle. Note the carved panel which bears the date 1576. Later additions to the building include the forestair, which was built against the south side of the tower in 1617, and the belfry, with its ogival roof, which was added in the 18th century.

How to get there:
O.S. Sheet 59 NT304931
Dysart lies adjacent to the east end of Kirkcaldy, on the A955 Kirkcaldy - Leven road. The tolbooth lies at the junction of High Street and Victoria Street in the centre of Dysart. Car parking is available either in the centre or nearby at the shore.

35. West Wemyss Tolbooth

West Wemyss became a burgh of barony in 1511 and by 1592 the burgh had its own small harbour, *tolbooth* and mercat cross. The original 16th century tolbooth was replaced by the present building at the beginning of the 18th century.

Built by David, 4th Earl of Wemyss (1678-1720), the tolbooth is a simple rectangular building, two storeys in height. A lofty bell tower which projects forward into the street must have been a source of civic pride. The tolbooth served as both jail and council chamber. The blocked entrances to the former prison cells may still be seen in the vaulted pend which passes through the western end of the building.

How to get there:
O.S. Sheet 59 NT325946
West Wemyss lies a short distance to the south of the main A955 Kirkcaldy - Leven road. The tolbooth is on the main street. Car parking is available at the end of the main street.

36. Inverkeithing Mercat Cross

Inverkeithing is an ancient royal burgh which was established in the 12th century. Its *mercat cross* was first erected in the 16th century and was originally placed at the north end of the High Street. It has since been moved twice, firstly to Townhall Street in 1799, and then again to its present position in Bank Street in 1974.

The mercat cross is a particularly fine example of its kind. A simple octagonal pillar rises from a stepped base and is surmounted by a carved capital bearing four heraldic shields. One of these shields depicts the arms of King Robert III (1390 - 1406) and another the arms of the Earl of Douglas. The cubical sundial and unicorn were added to the cross in 1688.

How to get there:
O.S. Sheet 65 NT130828
Bank Street is at the northern end of the High Street. Car parking is available on the High Street.

37. Crail Harbour

Crail Harbour is a small and picturesque haven which dates back to mediaeval times. As inhabitants of a royal burgh, the merchants of Crail were entitled to trade overseas and the trading vessels which once moored in the harbour must have brought considerable wealth to the little town.

The oldest part of the harbour is the south quay which was probably built in the late 15th or early 16th century. The west quay was added in the early 19th century when the harbour was once again a bustling centre - this time for the herring trade. The final improvements were made to the harbour in 1862, when booms were added to the entrance to protect the boats from stormy weather.

How to get there:
O.S. Sheet 59 NO611074
Vehicular access to the harbour is restricted, and cars should be parked elsewhere in the town, where there are a number of marked parking places. Access to the harbour is signed.

38. Culross Palace

Culross Palace is a magnificent example of a wealthy merchant's house. It was built between 1597 and 1611 by Sir George Bruce, a merchant who made his fortune from coal-mining and salt manufacture. Bruce eventually became a wealthy local land-owner by acquiring the estate of Carnock. This included most of the lands of the parishes of Culross and Carnock.

Bruce's mansion house is a picturesque building with white, harled walls, crow-stepped gables and pantiled roofs. It was built in stages and consists of four main blocks set around a large courtyard. The oldest part of the building is the central wing on the west side of the courtyard. This was built in 1597. The long gallery of the south wing was added in the early 17th century. The north range, with its kitchen and bakehouse, was also incorporated into the mansion at that time. A fourth, isolated range of buildings stands on the northern side of the courtyard. This is a curious building with a stable and byre in the lower floor and domestic accommodation above. The fine paintings which decorate the ceilings, walls and roof beams throughout the house are particularly worthy of note.

How to get there:
O.S. Sheet 65 NS985859
Culross lies on the north coast of the Firth of Forth, approximately mid way between Cairneyhill (5km west of Dunfermline) and Kincardine on the B9037. Car parking is available at the western end of Culross, just off the B9037. The palace is in the centre of Culross.

Location of Archaeological Sites

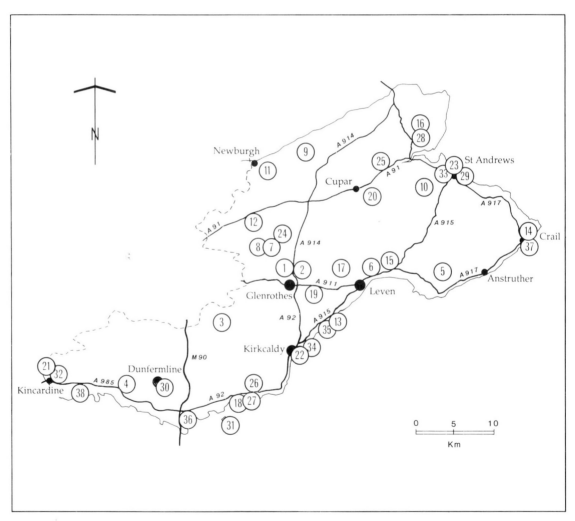

BIBLIOGRAPHY

Fawcett, R.:   Scottish Mediaeval Churches,   Edinburgh   1985

Gifford, J.:   The Buildings of Scotland: Fife   London   1988

Henderson, I.:   The Picts,   London   1967

Keppie L.:   Scotland's Roman Remains,   Edinburgh   1986

Mair, C.:   Mercat Cross and Tolbooth,   Edinburgh   1988

Ritchie, G and A.:   Scotland: Archaeology and Early History, London   1981

Tabraham, C.:   Scottish Castles and Fortifications,   Edinburgh   1986

Wainwright, F.T. (ed).: The Problem of the Picts,   Edinburgh   1955
                                                                 (Reprinted Perth 1980)

Walker, B. and   Exploring Scotland's Heritage:
Ritchie, G.:   Fife and Tayside,   Edinburgh   1987

Royal Commision on the
Ancient and Historical
Monuments of Scotland; Inventory of Monuments and
                         Constructions of Fife, Kinross
                         and Clackmannan,   Edinburgh 1933

Museums In Fife

The Scottish Fisheries Museum
St Ayles
Harbourhead
Anstruther

Crawford Centre for the Arts
University of St Andrews
93 North Street
St Andrews

Crail Museum and Heritage Centre
Marketgate
Crail

British Golf Museum
R & A Golf Club
St Andrews

Fife Folk Museum
Old High Street
Ceres
by Cupar

St Andrews University Archaeology
Museum
Swallowgate Building
St Andrews

Laing Museum
High Street
Newburgh

Dunfermline District Museum
Viewfield Terrace
Dunfermline

The St Andrews Preservation Trust Museum
12 North Street
St Andrews

Pittencrieff House Museum
Pittencrieff Park
Dunfermline